n-Avon

Shakespeare's debt to Stratford in giving him educa[tion]
acute awareness of nature is outweighed by the town's
in having the Birthplace and other properties as shrines for those
who love and revere him. Few visitors are disappointed by a town
where there are three theatres, a beautiful medieval church, and
many houses dating from the age of Shakespeare. The rare
atmosphere of Stratford will refresh the spirit and give an insight
into the most wonderful verse ever written in the English language.

Historic Stratford

There has been a settlement at the site of Stratford since the Bronze Age but it is only in the last few centuries that the town has found fame as the birthplace of Shakespeare. In the bard's day Stratford was a market town with streets that would often have been as bustling and colourful as those of London.

The name of the town gives a clue to its origins. Stratford-upon-Avon began as a settlement on the banks of the River Avon at a ford that was busy in Roman and Saxon times and had been in existence in the Bronze Age.

The 'Domesday Book' records Stratford as a manor – rather less than a village – belonging to the Bishop of Worcester, but by King John's reign this had grown into a thriving market town with a famous three-day fair attracting merchants from near and far. At about the same time a wooden bridge was built over the Avon and a start had been made on building the church.

Shakespeare's Stratford would have been a prosperous little place with merchants and tradesmen working under the protective Guild of the Holy Trinity that funded the Grammar School he attended. When he had made his fortune he bought a mansion in the town centre (New Place) and eventually retired there. Unhappily, his retirement lasted only six years and he died at New Place in 1616, probably after a convivial evening with fellow writers Ben Jonson and Michael Drayton.

Stratford's subsequent history reflects the growth of the poet's reputation after

TOP LEFT | *A view of the Avon and church in the early 1700s*

TOP RIGHT | *David Garrick 1717–1779*

LEFT | *The 1769 Shakespearian Festival at the Birthplace*

RIGHT | *An angel carved for the medieval guild*

his death. This gathered pace after the Shakespearian Festival organised by the famous actor David Garrick in 1769. Visitors flocked to see the Birthplace but pieces were

ABOVE I *The Birthplace as an inn (19th century)*
RIGHT I *The Shakespeare Centre*
BOTTOM RIGHT I *Henley Street today*

hacked off the poet's famous chair and sold as souvenirs. Vandalism like this threatened Shakespeare's heritage but this began to be safeguarded when the Birthplace was purchased for £3,000 in 1847 with money raised by public subscription. This was the

beginning of the Trust that now administers the five Shakespeare properties. An exhibition at the Shakespeare Centre, next to the Birthplace, illustrates its history.

In 1864 there was a second festival to celebrate the tri-centenary of Shakespeare's birth. These celebrations fostered the idea of a memorial theatre and this was realised some years later. Hotels were built to cater for visitors whose numbers increased further when the railway reached Stratford in 1859.

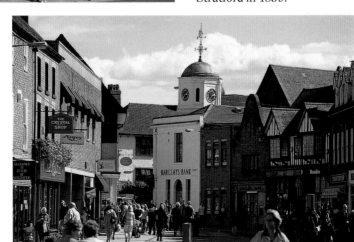

LEFT | *Palmer's Farm, Wilmcote – once thought to be the home of Shakespeare's mother*

BELOW | *The room where Shakespeare was born*

RIGHT | *Anne Hathaway's Cottage at Shottery*

BELOW RIGHT | *Engraving of Shakespeare on First Folio of the plays, 1623*

William Shakespeare

The 'Sweet Swan of Avon' was born and died in Stratford but spent most of his life in London, building a reputation as playwright and poet that shines even more brightly today.

John Shakespeare, William's father, was a well-known figure in Stratford when William was born on 23 April 1564. He was an important official in local government and also acted as a merchant for local farmers. More importantly, he had married into money. His wife Mary was the daughter of Robert Arden, a farmer at Wilmcote and thus the Shakespeare's were well respected in the town, with John becoming an alderman when William was about four years old.

In 1571 the boy was enrolled at the Grammar School where he studied for six years, mainly learning Latin. When he left school he worked for a time with his father whose business

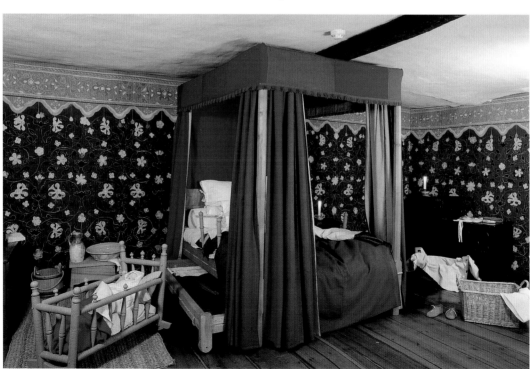

was failing (he was deprived of the office of alderman in 1586 because of debt). At the age of 18 William married Anne Hathaway – probably a 'shotgun' wedding since Anne presented him with a daughter six months later.

In 1585 she produced twins, Hamnet and Judith. That same year Shakespeare abruptly left Stratford and his family. His departure is usually supposed to be due to a charge of deer poaching that had been brought against him by Sir Thomas Lucy of Charlecote. His revenge against the pompous landowner and magistrate was sweet – Justice Shallow in *Henry IV Part 2* and *The Merry Wives of Windsor* is said to be a caricature of Lucy.

It seems likely that Shakespeare became a village schoolmaster for a short time before reaching London. Either by accident or design he gained employment at one of the capital's leading theatres, initially working as a jack-of-all-trades. Perhaps his acting talent as an extra led to him being engaged by the Earl of Leicester's company of actors who performed at famous venues like the Rose and the Globe. The company soon made use of Shakespeare's aptitude with the pen, initially by editing and rewriting other people's work, but then by producing his own plays.

One of the first of these was *Love's Labour's Lost*, written in 1591 and performed at court for Queen Elizabeth's pleasure in 1597. Shakespeare was a prolific writer and though he began by writing a series of comedies, he was soon producing tragedies as well, with the occasional patriotic history play thrown in for good measure. The last decade of the 16th century must have been a rousing one for Shakespeare, working with

actors whom he admired and with writers like Ben Jonson and Christopher Marlowe, who became his drinking companions. Could he have had time during these hectic years to compose the passionate sonnets and love poems as well? The argument as to whether Shakespeare was truly the author of these has raged for more than a hundred years and is still unresolved.

By 1597 Shakespeare had

become a wealthy man and was able to return to Stratford to redeem his father's debts. While he was there he purchased the largest house in the town, New Place. His visit was probably brief, and he was soon back in London writing more plays.

The last work that can be attributed to Shakespeare with certainty was *The Tempest*, written in 1611. By this time he had retired to Stratford, though he still made frequent visits to London to oversee the publication of his work and attend productions of plays that either he, or his friends, had written. In 1613 he bought a house in Blackfriars where he could stay on these occasions and he also took more property at Stratford. He courted unpopularity by trying to enclose common land at Stratford but was unsuccessful.

After 1614 Shakespeare stopped going to London and settled down to a peaceful and uneventful life in the town of his birth. He was probably in declining health, as in January 1616 he drafted his will, signing it about a month

The Globe

before his death. On 22 April he entertained his old friends Ben Jonson and Michael Drayton at New Place, where he died the following day. His wife Anne lived until 1623, and his last relation to survive was his granddaughter Elizabeth Hall who died in 1670. New Place was sold in 1675 and later came into the hands of the local vicar. He became so fed up with visitors asking to see the home of Shakespeare that he had the house demolished in 1759.

FAR LEFT | *William Shakespeare, attributed to Pieter Borseller, c.1660–70 (The Chesterfield Portrait)*

ABOVE | *A scene from* The Comedy of Errors *at The Globe*

BOTTOM LEFT | *Visscher's panorama of 1616 shows The Globe on the right*

BELOW | *The reconstructed Globe Theatre, Bankside, London*

GOOD FREND FOR IESVS SAKE FORBEARE,
TO DIGG THE DVST ENCLOASED HEARE:
BLESTE BE Y MAN Y SPARES THES STONES,
AND CVRST BE HE Y MOVES MY BONES.

Important Dates in the Life and Times of Shakespeare

1558 Elizabeth I became Queen of England
1564 William Shakespeare baptised on 26 April
Birth of Galileo, inventor of the telescope
1568 John Shakespeare elected Bailiff of Stratford
1575 Queen Elizabeth visited Kenilworth Castle
1577 Drake sailed round the world
Holinshed's *Chronicles of England, Scotland and Ireland* first published
1582 Shakespeare married Anne Hathaway
1583 Birth of Shakespeare's daughter Susanna
1585 Birth of Hamnet and Judith, Shakespeare's twins
1587 Execution of Mary Queen of Scots
1588 Defeat of the Spanish Armada
1592 Production of Shakespeare's *Henry VI, Part 1*
1593 Publication of Shakespeare's *Venus and Adonis*
Death of Christopher Marlowe
1594 Shakespeare joined the Lord Chamberlain's company
1595 Raleigh's expedition to South America
1596 Burial of Hamnet Shakespeare
Grant of Arms to John Shakespeare
1597 Shakespeare purchased New Place
1599 Opening of the Globe Theatre, Bankside
1600 East India Company formed
1601 Burial of the poet's father
1602 Shakespeare purchased land in Old Stratford
Bodleian Library at Oxford opened
1603 Florio's translation of *Montaigne* published
Death of Queen Elizabeth I and accession of King James I
1605 The Gunpowder Plot headed by Guy Fawkes
Shakespeare purchased a lease of the tithes of Stratford
1607 First English Settlement in Jamestown, Virginia
Susanna Shakespeare married Dr John Hall
1608 Birth of Elizabeth Hall, Shakespeare's granddaughter
Death of the poet's mother
1609 First edition of Shakespeare's *Sonnets* printed
1610 Shakespeare retired to New Place
1613 The Globe Theatre destroyed by fire
1616 Death of Shakespeare on 23 April
1618 Beginning of the Thirty Years' War
1623 First Folio edition of Shakespeare's plays published

Shakespeare Houses

In the 19th century visitors to Stratford carved their names into woodwork and furniture and scrawled on the ceilings. To safeguard properties connected with the bard for future generations, five were bought by the Shakespeare Birthplace Trust, which still cares for them today.

Shakespeare's Birthplace in Henley Street has served many purposes over the centuries. At the time of William's birth in 1564 it belonged to his father, John, a well-respected and prosperous townsman. Before his marriage he was a glover and probably continued this craft at the house. The Shakespeares actually lived in just half of the house seen today, the other half served as a store for bales of wool and as a shop and workroom for glovemaking. William was the third child and there were to be five more so the house would have been lively and crowded. Meanwhile, John Shakespeare continued to pursue his civic responsibilities – he became Bailiff of Stratford in 1568, a position roughly equivalent of mayor.

When Shakespeare retired to Stratford in 1610 he lived in a medieval house known as **New Place**. This was pulled down in the 18th century and only the foundations survive.

TOP | *Shakespeare's Birthplace*
LEFT | *Hall's Croft*

They may be viewed by visiting beautiful **Nash's House** in Chapel Street, the home of Shakespeare's granddaughter Elizabeth who married Thomas Nash. Like the other Shakespearian properties it has outstanding furniture of the period as well as interesting exhibits of local history. One of the most colourful sights of Stratford is the intricate replica of an Elizabethan Knot Garden that occupies part of the site of New Place. The lower part of the garden – the orchard and kitchen garden of the house in Shakespeare's time – is open to the public (access in Chapel Lane) and is maintained by the Birthplace Trust as a delightful memorial of the bard.

Hall's Croft is in Old Town close to Holy Trinity Church. It takes its name from Dr John Hall who came to the house when he married Susanna, Shakespeare's favourite daughter. His pharmacy and consulting room may be seen by visitors, and herbs that might have been used in his remedies grow in the enclosed gardens.

ABOVE LEFT | *The dispensary at Hall's Croft*
ABOVE RIGHT | *Nash's House*
BELOW | *Gardens at New Place*

Turn left as you leave the Centre to pass Shakespeare's Birthplace where he entered the world on 23 April 1564. Turn right into High Street at the roundabout, passing the former Market House with its clock tower (1821) on the right at the end of Wood Street. Judith Shakespeare, the poet's daughter born in 1585, lived in a house opposite on the Bridge Street corner. Harvard House is on the right hand side of High Street. It was built after Stratford's Great Fire of 1595 by Thomas Rogers. His daughter married Robert Harvard of Southwark and their son founded the American university. The adjoining Garrick Inn is also picturesque with its jettied upper storey.

Keep ahead at the top of Sheep Street to pass the Town Hall which dates from 1767. This is Chapel Street and the bank building on the right has terracotta illustrations from Shakespeare's plays. The Shakespeare Hotel is to the left

A Town Walk

The walk starts from the Shakespeare Centre in Henley Street.

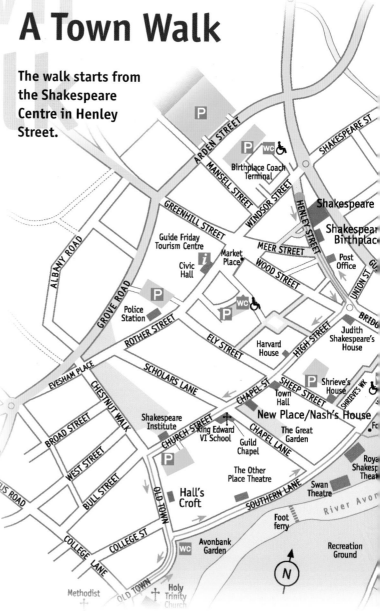

(above) – it incorporates 16th- and late 17th-century houses and became a hotel in early Victorian times. A house on the site of the Chaucer's Head Bookshop was the home of Julius Shaw, Shakespeare's friend and a witness to his will. Nash's House *(right)* is the last

building before Chapel Lane. It was the home of Thomas Nash who married Elizabeth Hall, Shakespeare's granddaughter. New Place stood on the corner next to Nash's House. The 15th-century mansion was bought by Shakespeare in 1597 and he lived there from 1610 until his death on 23 April 1616. Visitors to Nash's House can see the intricate Knot and herb gardens,

Tramway Bridge is a fine viewpoint for the river and for the medieval Clopton Bridge upstream.

Croft is on the left, home of John Hall who married Susanna, Shakespeare's elder daughter, in 1607. Keep ahead towards the crossroads to reach Holy Trinity church *(below right)* where Shakespeare is buried. Return along Old Town and turn right into Southern Lane. After the Other Place Theatre there is a chain ferry on the right crossing to the meadows on the south bank of the Avon. The Swan and Royal Shakespeare Theatres *(above)* are on the right after the Black Swan inn ('Dirty Duck') on

HEERE LYETH INTERRED THE BODY OF ANNE WIFE OF WILLIAM SHAKESPEARE, WHO DEPTED THIS LIFE THE 6 DAY OF AVGV 1623 BEING OF THE AGE OF 67 YEARES

Vbera, tu mater, tu lac, vitamq dedisti
Væ mihi pro tanto munere saxa dabo
Quam mallem amoueat lapidem, bonus angl? ore
Exeat christi corpus, imago tua
Sed nil vota valent venias cito Christe refurget
Clausa licet tumulo mater et astra petet

the left. Take the path by the fountain into the gardens on the right and cross the footbridge over the river end of the canal basin *(top right)*. Cox's Yard complex faces you at the end of the footpath. To the right, the

To return to the Birthplace turn left and pass the famous Gower Memorial, where characters from the plays surround a statue of Shakespeare. Walk up Bridge Street to the roundabout and then bear slightly right to Henley Street and the starting point.

but access to the lower part of the Great Garden is free (gate on Chapel Lane).

Keep ahead into Church Street passing the Guild Chapel and King Edward VI School *(right)*. Shakespeare attended the grammar school run by the Guild in the upper floor of the 15th-century half-timbered building. Almshouses of the same period come after the school.

Turn left at the end of Church Street into Old Town. Hall's

More properties connected with Shakespeare and his family lie on the outskirts of Stratford.

Anne Hathaway's Cottage is at Shottery, within walking distance of the town. With its old-fashioned gardens and orchard, the cottage is one of the best-known buildings in the world and has the added attraction of being where Shakespeare came to woo his bride-to-be.

The cottage dates from the 15th century and is surprisingly large. Built on stone foundations, the oldest part has a timber framework using a cruck truss, the walls being of puddled mud and wattles finished with horse-hair plaster. This was the traditional form of construction in medieval times. Visitors can climb narrow stairs to see the

famous Hathaway bedstead with its rich woodcarving. The kitchen and dairy downstairs and the six upstairs rooms give a wonderful insight as to how life was lived in a country farmhouse four centuries ago.

Slightly further from town at Wilmcote but almost equally picturesque is **Palmer's Farm**, until recently thought to have been the home of Mary Arden, Shakespeare's mother. It now turns out that she was actually brought up at the adjacent property, formerly known as Glebe Farm, and this is the true **Mary Arden's House**. Both farmhouses are open to the public and though Mary Arden's House may look modest from the outside, the interior dates from *c.* 1514, which makes it slightly older than Palmer's Farm. Visitors will see a collection of domestic and agricultural bygones as well as real animals in the farmyard.

FAR LEFT | *Anne Hathaway's Cottage, Shottery*

ABOVE | *Mary Arden's House, Wilmcote*

BELOW | *Palmer's Farm, formerly known as Mary Arden's House*

The first production of a Shakespeare play in Stratford took place in 1746, 130 years after the poet's death. Today a season of his plays can be seen each year at the Royal Shakespeare Theatre while two other theatres offer alternative drama.

The Theatres

In 1769 the famous London actor David Garrick staged a lavish Shakespeare festival at Stratford, the centrepiece being his recitations of famous speeches from the plays. Strangely none of these were performed at the time, and although the festival succeeded in putting Stratford in the limelight it was not until 1879 that the first memorial theatre was opened on the bank of the Avon. Since then Stratford has never been without a season of Shakespearian drama.

The present memorial theatre dates from 1932 and was designed by Elizabeth Scott. A new auditorium retains the key Art Deco and Victorian elements of the existing building, whilst creating a more intimate and contemporary setting for the performance of Shakespeare's plays in the 21st century.

Many famous actors have begun their careers at Stratford, and most of them have returned at the peak of their fame to appear again.

The productions of the Royal Shakespeare Company have become benchmarks of excellence and are taken abroad as tokens of British culture. The company performs in various theatres in London.

The Swan Theatre, opened in 1986 and attached to the Royal Shakespeare Theatre, has an Elizabethan-style stage where plays written by Shakespeare's peers are produced. It is built within the shell of the former memorial theatre. On the other side of the road, towards Holy Trinity church, The Courtyard Theatre will be used for the World Shakespeare Festival in 2012.

Theatre tours take place on most days through the season and illustrate how plays are staged as well as the history of theatre production at Stratford.

ABOVE and LEFT | *The Royal Shakespeare Theatre built in 1932, with a new auditorium in 2010*

ABOVE | *On stage at the Royal Shakespeare Theatre*
BELOW LEFT | *The Other Place Theatre*
BELOW | *The Swan Theatre*

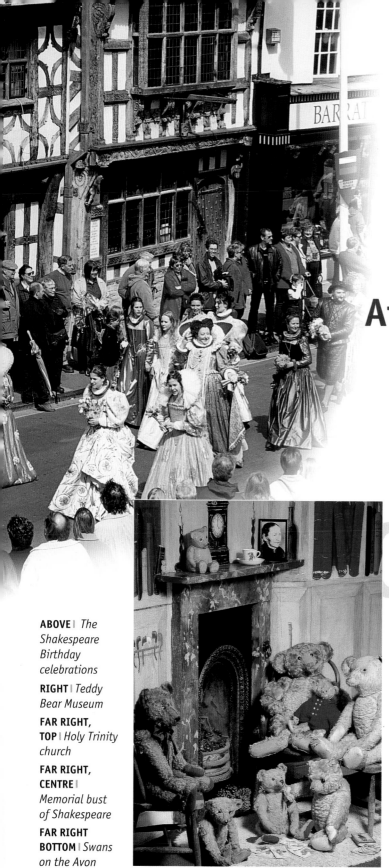

Tourist interest is inevitably focused on Shakespeare at Stratford, but there are other attractions to entertain the visitor.

Other Attractions

The Saturday nearest to April 23 is the day when Stratford celebrates its greatest son each year with an extravagant birthday party. Diplomats from many countries join actors, civic leaders and schoolchildren in a procession from the Birthplace to Holy Trinity church where they lay floral tributes by his tomb. At the same times banners and national flags are unfurled along the streets. Stratford's parish church dates from the time when the town began to expand from being a tiny village to a busy medieval market town. Its best architectural features are the 15th-century chancel and clerestory, but most people come to see the monument and tomb of Shakespeare. However there are countless other interesting features that are often overlooked, like the

ABOVE | *The Shakespeare Birthday celebrations*

RIGHT | *Teddy Bear Museum*

FAR RIGHT, TOP | *Holy Trinity church*

FAR RIGHT, CENTRE | *Memorial bust of Shakespeare*

FAR RIGHT BOTTOM | *Swans on the Avon*

600-year-old font where he was baptised or the Clopton Chapel with its splendid monuments.

There are good views of the church from the River Avon and a popular summer pastime is to hire a boat to row downstream to the weir or paddle in a canoe upstream to Clopton Bridge and beyond. Passenger boats also provide trips, while a canal boat serves as a floating restaurant, cruising while diners eat. Children enjoy feeding ducks and swans by the riverside and will also appreciate the Museum of Teddy Bears in Greenhill Street and the Butterfly Farm on Tramway Walk. Finally, an evening stroll along the south bank of the Avon to see the sun setting behind Holy Trinity church will become a treasured memory of a romantic town.

The architecture of **Ragley Hall** *(left)*, near Alcester, is classical – the original house having been built by Robert Hooke for the Earl of Conway at the end of the 18th century. It was subsequently enlarged and enhanced by Wyatt and Gibbs, the latter mainly responsible for creating the stunning baroque interior.

Many people only go to Royal Leamington Spa *(below)* to visit its excellent shops, but its elegant Regency buildings and spacious gardens give it a special atmosphere.

Surrounding Area

Stratford lies at the heart of England and many castles, historic houses and famous gardens are within easy reach. Newcomers to the area can also explore places like Leamington Spa with its Regency buildings or Coventry, a medieval city bombed but resurrected.

Although Leamington's waters were found to be beneficial in the 16th century, the town only developed as a spa after 1800, reaching its heyday when Queen Victoria gave it royal status in 1838.

Beautiful **Coughton Court** has been the home of the Throckmorton family since the early 15th century *(below)*. Parts of the house date from this time but it is a building that has seen many alterations over the centuries. Since the family remained staunchly Catholic through the reigns of Mary and Elizabeth it suffered many penalties and the house is full of hiding-places for the priests of that time.

Hidcote Manor Garden *(top left)* was designed by an American, Lawrence Johnston, as a patchwork of 'rooms' that give a uniquely satisfying result. It is often acclaimed as the most influential

20th-century garden. Hidcote belongs to the National Trust and is about thirty minutes' drive south of Stratford.

Warwick *(top)* is about the same distance to the north of the town, its wonderful castle commanding the surrounding countryside from a bluff above the River Avon. Only Windsor can rival its magnificent effect, but visitors will see more at Warwick. The parish church, with the incomparable Beauchamp Chapel, and the picturesque Lord

Leycester Hospital provide further reason for exploring the town.

Charlecote Park *(above)* lies much closer to Stratford and is where, legend has it, Shakespeare was caught trying to poach deer and hauled before the local magistrate, Sir Thomas Lucy. Lucy built the original house and the gatehouse survives of this era though the remainder is largely Victorian. The Lucys have held land at Charlecote for more than 700 years and the family still occupies the house.

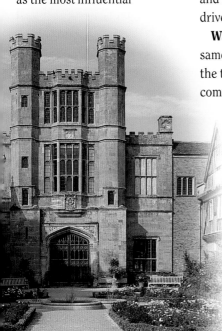

impression that has not dulled with the years. Around the cathedral a new city is rising, some of it replacing the first rebuilding of the 1960s.

Packwood House *(below)*, a National Trust property to the north of Stratford, has wonderful gardens that offer a complete contrast to those at Hidcote. The house itself is Elizabethan and the Great Hall has a chimneypiece that originally belonged to a Stratford inn. This is because the hall and the long gallery were added in the 1920s. However, it is the gardens

A new **Coventry Cathedral** *(above and left)* was built to replace the medieval one destroyed by bombing in the Second World War. It was consecrated in 1962, having been built to the designs of Sir Basil Spence. Inside, the vast tapestry by Graham Sutherland leaves an